a
animals

Trace **a**. Then write **a**.

Write **a** to finish the picture words.

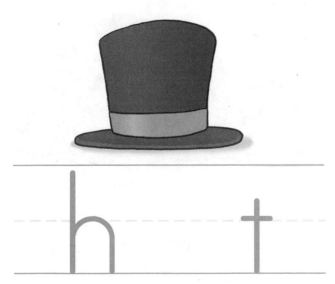

_h t

_ n t

1

b

bird

Trace **b**. Then write **b**.

Write **b** to finish the picture words.

ba___y

___ear

2

C

camel

Trace **c**. Then write **c**.

Write **c** to finish the picture words.

at

ar

d
dog

Trace **d**. Then write **d**.

Write **d** to finish the picture words.

oll

be

4

e

elephant

Trace e. Then write e.

Write e to finish the picture words.

gg

b   ll

f

fox

Trace **f**. Then write **f**.

Write **f** to finish the picture words.

 ___ish

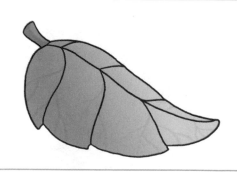 ___lea

6

g

goose

Trace **g**. Then write **g**.

Write **g** to finish the picture words.

 irl

 wa on

h

helmets

Trace **h**. Then write **h**.

Write **h** to finish the picture words.

___at

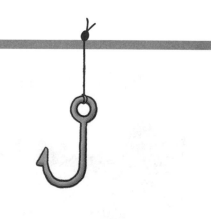

___ook

i
insects

Trace **i**. Then write **i**.

2 ◆
1 ↓

Write **i** to finish the picture words.

f _ sh

_ gloo

j
jaguar

Trace j. Then write j.

j

Write j to finish the picture words.

am

et

10

k
kangaroos

Trace **k**. Then write **k**.

Write **k** to finish the picture words.

_ey

_boo

l

lizard

Trace **l**. Then write **l**.

Write **l** to finish the picture words.

_____ ion

_____ ow

m

moose

Trace **m**. Then write **m**.

im

Write **m** to finish the picture words.

ouse

dru

n

numbers

Trace **n**. Then write **n**.

Write **n** to finish the picture words.

bar

est

octopus

Trace o. Then write o.

Write o to finish the picture words.

_ x

s _ ck

p

penguins

Trace **p**. Then write **p**.

Write **p** to finish the picture words.

_ig

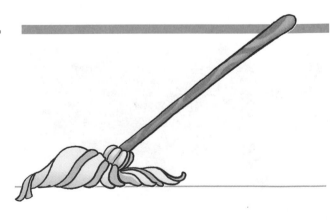

mo_

16

q

quail

Trace **q**. Then write **q**.

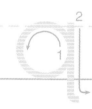

Write **q** to finish the picture words.

uilt

ueen

r

rocket

Trace **r**. Then write **r**.

Write **r** to finish the picture words.

___ake

bi___d

18

s
seal

Trace **s**. Then write **s**.

Write **s** to finish the picture words.

 un

 va_e

t

turtle

Trace t. Then write t.

Write t to finish the picture words.

op

ba

20

u
umbrellas

Trace **u**. Then write **u**.

Write **u** to finish the picture words.

p

b g

V

valentines

Trace **v**. Then write **v**. ▬▬▬▬▬▬

Write **v** to finish the picture words. ▬▬▬▬▬

f i _ e   ri _ er

W

watermelon

Trace **w**. Then write **w**.

Write **w** to finish the picture words.

_orm   _co

X

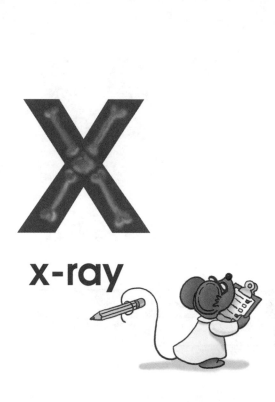

x-ray

Trace **x**. Then write **x**.

Write **x** to finish the picture words.

fo___

si___

y

yarn

Trace y. Then write y.

Write y to finish the picture words.

o- o

a k

Z
zipper

Trace **z**. Then write **z**.

Write **z** to finish the picture words.

ero

ebra

26

Write the correct **letter** to finish each picture word.

e   d   r

b _ ll

bi _ d

_ og

Write the correct **letter** to finish each picture word.

p a h

c   t

mo

ook

Write the correct **letter** to finish each picture word.

c   m   o

fr __ g

dru __

__ ar

Write the correct **letter** to finish each picture word.

_ ear

f _ sh

hor _ e

Write the correct **letter** to finish each picture word.

w u l

b _ g

_ ion

c o _

Double Vision

Circle the pictures that are the **same** size.

Bigger Bugs

Circle the picture that is **bigger** than the first one.

Best Pets

Circle the picture that is **smaller** than the first one.

Long Legs

Circle the bird with the **long** pants.

Circle the bird with the **long** legs.

Heads and Tails

Circle the dog with the **short** tail.

Circle the child with **short** hair.

Match the Clothes

These are the **same**.

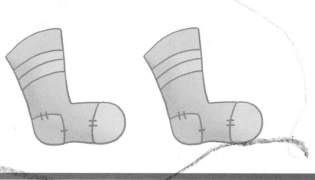

Circle 2 that are the **same**.

Find the Match

Circle 2 that are the **same**.

What Is Different?

One is **different**.

Circle the picture that is **different**.

40

Different Animals

Circle the picture that is **different**.

What Goes Together?

 belongs with

Circle the picture that **belongs** with the first one.

 |

 |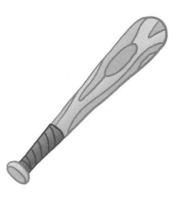

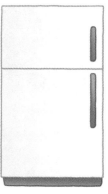 |

42

What Goes Together?

Circle the picture that **belongs** with the first one.

What Goes Together?

Circle the picture that **belongs** with the first one.

What Goes Together?

Circle the picture that **belongs** with the first one.

Beautiful Blue

Color the  blue.

Color what is blue.

46

Yippee for Yellow

Color the  yellow.

Color what is yellow.

Real Red

Color the 🍎 **red**.

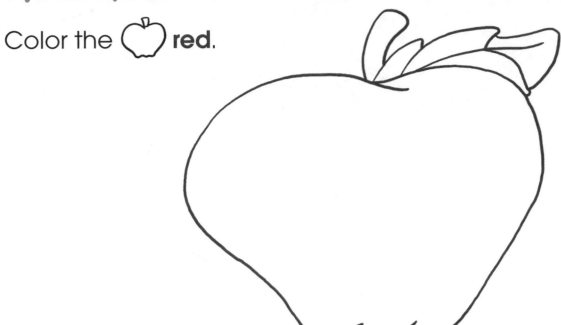

Color what is **red**.

48

Perfect Purple

Color the 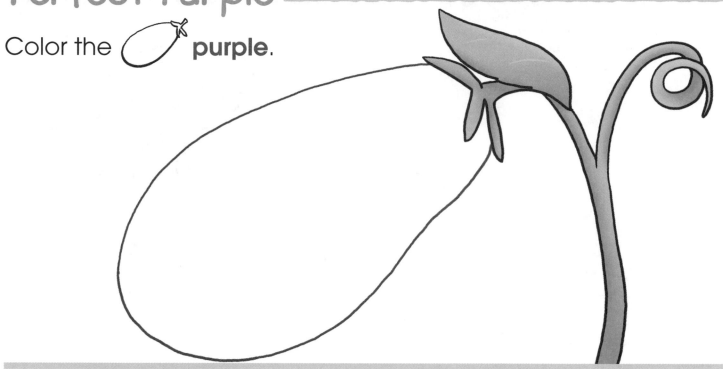 **purple**.

Color what is **purple**.

Outstanding Orange

Color the  orange.

Color what is **orange**.

Green Is Great

Color the  green.

Color what is **green**.

All of the Colors

Color the 🌳 green.

Color the ☀ yellow.

Color the 〰 blue.

Color the ⛵ orange.

Color the ☂ red.

Color the 🏠 purple.

52

53

Summer Fun

Circle what you would wear.

54

Let It Snow

Circle what you would wear.

Where Does It Belong?

 **belong** in a 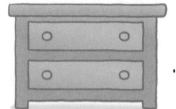 .

Draw a line to where each thing **belongs**.

56

Which Store?

Draw a line to where each thing **belongs**.

Where Does It Belong?

Draw a line to where each thing **belongs**.

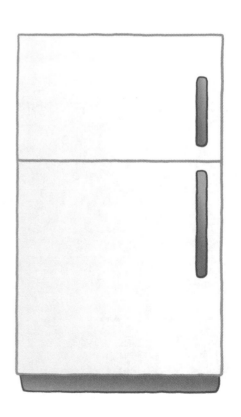

How Would You Feel?

 happy

 sad

Circle the face that shows how you would **feel**.

Pond Patterns

Color the last one in each row to finish the pattern.

60

Find the Opposite

in

out

Circle the picture that shows the **opposite** of the first one.

up

night

big

Find the Opposite

Circle the picture that shows the **opposite** of the first one.

empty

hot

dry

Beginning Sounds

penguin   pizza

Circle the picture that begins with the **same sound** as the first one.

monkey

bird

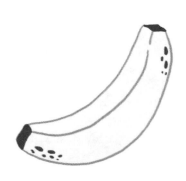

pig

Beginning Sounds

Circle the picture that begins with the **same sound** as the first one.

turkey

ladder

nest

Beginning Sounds

Circle the picture that begins with the **same sound** as the first one.

dog

horse

fish

66

Beginning Sounds

Circle the picture that begins with the **same sound** as the first one.

kangaroo

wagon

cat

Beginning Sounds

Circle the picture that begins with the **same sound** as the first one.

zebra

alligator

octopus

68

Beginning Sounds

Circle the picture that begins with
the **same sound** as the first one.

goat

rabbit

sun

Fresh from the Bakery

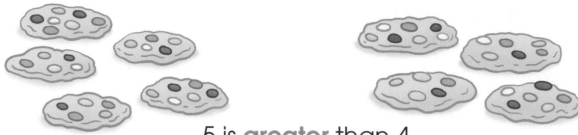

5 is **greater** than 4.

Circle the group that is **greater**.

School Fun

2 is **less** than 3.

Circle the group that has **less**.

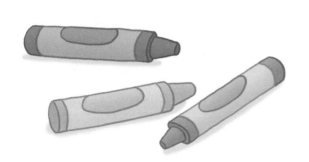 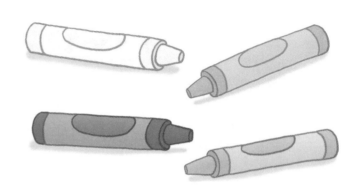

Rhyme Time

 **rhymes** with  .

Circle the picture that **rhymes** with the first one.

 |

 |

 |

More Rhymes

Circle the picture that **rhymes** with the first one.

At Home

 **one**

Circle everything that there is only **one** of below.

On the Farm

2
two

Circle the groups of **2**.

Road Trip

3
three

Circle the groups of 3.

A Day at the Beach

4
four

Circle the groups of **4**.

Toyland

5
five

Circle the groups of **5**.

Happy Birthday

6
six

Circle the groups of 6.

Outdoor Friends

7
seven

Circle the groups of 7.

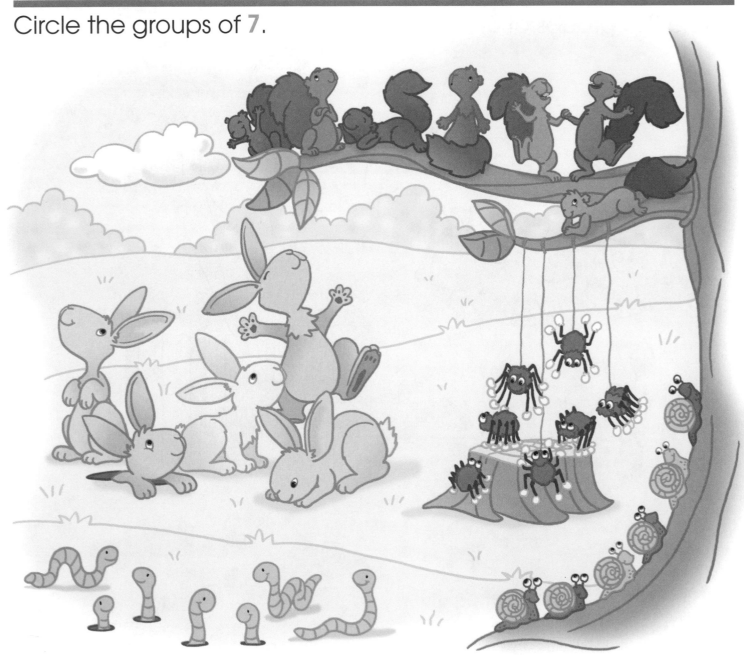

Busy Bugs

8
eight

Circle the groups of **8**.

Ocean Animals

9
nine

Circle the groups of 9.

Life at the Pond

10
ten

Circle the groups of **10**.

What Is in the Yard?

How many of each are on both pages?
Circle the number.

trees	**2**	**3**	**4**
dogs	**2**	**3**	**4**
birds	**3**	**4**	**5**
houses	**1**	**2**	**3**

How many of each are on both pages?
Circle the number.

🍎s	6	7	8
🌼s	7	8	9
🦋s	4	5	6
🐝s	8	9	10

Count the Animals

Circle the group that shows the **same** number as the first one.

One More

Circle the group that shows **one more** than the first picture.

One Less

Circle the group that shows **one less** than the first picture.

Count the Toys

Circle the number that shows **how many**.

1   2   3   1   2   3

1   2   3   3   4   5

Count the Fruit

Circle the number that shows **how many**.

4   5   6

4   5   6

3   4   5

5   6   7

Sound It Out

Say the picture words.

Circle the picture word that begins with the same sound.

 **A** apple		
 **B** barn		
 **C** carrot		
 **D** dog		

TRY IT!

Draw a large boat. Write A, B, C, and D on the boat. Cut out pictures of things that begin with each of the letters, and then glue the pictures to the boat.

Calling All Sounds!

Say the picture words.

Circle the picture word that begins with the same sound.

 E eggs   

 F fish   

 G goat   

 H horse   

TRY IT!

Play animal alphabet with a friend. Name an animal and ask your friend to think of something else that begins with the same letter as the animal's name.

The Farm

1.
one

Circle 1
Circle 1
Circle 1

TRY IT!
Help your parents set the table for a meal. Count how many people will be there. Set one plate for each person. Then place one glass or cup for each person.

Visit the Animals

Follow the numbers from 1 to 9.
Draw a —— on the path.

Pond

Chicken Coop

Vegetable Garden

Pig Pen

FARM FUNNIES • FARM FUNNIES •

What keys won't open doors?

Turkeys!

Field

7

Cow Barn

Stable

6

8

5

Turkey Pen

9

Rabbit Hutch

TRY IT!
Draw a map of your room. Draw where your bed is located. Draw other things in your room, such as the door, your toy box, or your closet.

The Cow Barn

2 ..
two

Circle 2 s

Circle 2 s

Circle 2 s

FARM FUNNIES

Why did the farmer feed his cow money?

He wanted rich milk!

The Garden

3...
three

Circle 3 🐸 s

Circle 3 🐦 s

Circle 3 🐞 s

TRY IT!

Does your family have a garden?
How is your garden the same as
a farm? How is it different?

Around the Bend

This is a circle.

Color two circles **blue**.

Ducks

98

Say It Loud

Say the picture words.

Circle the picture word that begins with the same sound.

I ice cream

J jelly

K kite

L leaf

TRY IT!

Think of words that start with each letter of the alphabet to make up silly animal descriptions. For instance, "giddy goose," "messy mouse," or "purple, picky pig."

Barnyard Colors

Color the pictures.

FARM FUNNIES · FARM FUNNIES · FARM FUNNIES

Why do cows wear bells?

Because their horns don't work!

100

TRY IT!

What is your favorite color? Try to find as many things as you can that are that color. Cut out pictures from a magazine, look in your refrigerator, and find clothes in your closet.

The Field

4 ∷
four

Circle 4 🟫s

Circle 4 🐰s

Circle 4 🛒s

TRY IT! ♫ ♪
Make up a song without using any words. Clap your hands, stomp your feet, and snap your fingers!

The Stable

5 ⚫⚫
⚫
⚫⚫
five

Circle 5 s

Circle 5 s

Circle 5

FEED

FARM FUNNIES · FARM FUNNIES

What animal always goes to bed with its shoes on?

A horse!

The Farm House

6 ⠿
six

Circle 6 s

Circle 6 s

TRY IT!

You can make a funny-face snack. Cut a slice of
bread into a circle. Cover it with peanut butter.
Make a face using carrot curls, nuts, cheese, apples,
or raisins for the eyes, ears, nose, and mouth.

104

Square Dance

This is a square.

Color two squares **red**.

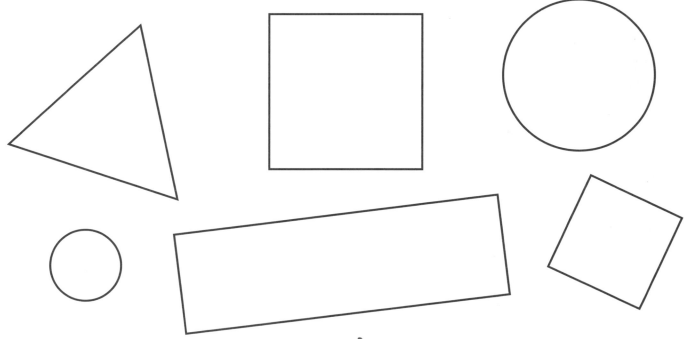

TRY IT!

Play a rhyming game. Open a magazine or a book with pictures. Point to a picture and say its name. Then say as many rhyming words as you can, even if they are nonsense words. For example, if you see a tree, you could say **bee**, **key**, and **gee**!

Home Sweet Home

This is a triangle. ▲

Color two triangles green.

TRY IT!

Fold a piece of paper in half. Draw a dotted line diagonally from a corner on the fold to a corner on the edge. Cut along the dotted line. When you unfold the paper, it will be in the shape of a triangle. Try cutting different lines to change the shape.

The Hen House

7 ⚫⚫⚫⚫⚫⚫⚫
seven

Circle 7 🪹 s
Circle 7 🐤 s

TRY IT!
Gather four fruits and vegetables. Line them up according to size. Which is the largest? Which is the smallest?

The Pond

8 eight

Circle 8 's
Circle 8 's

108

The Fairgrounds

9
nine

Circle 9 🚩 s

Circle 9 🍦 s

ICE CREAM

TRY IT!
Ask a grown-up to help you type the numbers from 1 to 9 on the computer. Print out the numbers, and then practice reading them.

Shaping Up

This is a rectangle.

Color two rectangles orange.

TRY IT!

Use blocks and a board to build a ramp. Roll a toy car down the ramp to see how far it goes. Add more blocks to the ramp and roll the car again. Does it roll the same distance?

Great Shape

Color the picture.

▭s **red**.

△s green.

◯s yellow.

▢s **blue**.

Shoo, Crows!

Use a to measure each scarecrow.

How many s tall is each one?

1. ☐

2. ☐

3. ☐

TRY IT!

Ask a grown-up to cut a piece of string about 12 inches long. Look around your home and guess which things are the same length as the string. Then use the string to check your guesses.

Match the Sounds

Say the picture words.

Circle the picture word that begins with the same sound.

  **M**
mouse

 **N**
nest

 **O**
ostrich

P
pig

TRY IT!

Write a letter of the alphabet on each square of a hopscotch grid. Toss a stone on a square, hop on the square, and say the letter or a word that begins with the letter. Then pick up the stone and hop back.

Sound Roundup

Say the picture words.

Circle the picture word that begins with the same sound.

 Q
quilt

 R
rabbit

 S
socks

 T
turkey

TRY IT!

Go on an alphabet hunt! Pick a letter of the alphabet. Then look in an old newspaper or magazine to find names that begin with the letter. Circle the names with a marker or crayon.

Pick a Pen

Draw a —— from each set of sheep to the correct pen.

TRY IT!

Play an imaginary animal game. Combine two animal names into one. For instance, a puppy combined with a hamster could be a pupster. What are the silliest combinations you can think of? Draw the wackiest animals.

Apple Trees

Draw 🍎s on each tree.

Draw as many as you want.

How many 🍎s? ⬜

FARM FUNNIES • FARM FUNNIES •

What kind of apple isn't an apple?

A pineapple

How many 🍎s?

How many 🍎s in all (🌳 + 🌳)?

Look at All the Babies!

How many of each kind of baby?

S [ ]

S [ ]

S [ ]

S [ ]

Suppose a farmer could raise an imaginary animal, such as a dragon or a unicorn. What kind of food would the farmer provide? Where would the animal live? Would it need special care?

How many of each kind of baby?

Count the Animals

Count how many are on both pages.
Circle the number.

ducks	4	5	6
frogs	1	2	3
butterflies	6	7	8

Count how many are on both pages.
Circle the number.

cow s	2	3	4
bird s	5	6	7
sheep	1	2	3

TRY IT!

Make the sounds of different animals. Moo like a cow. Oink like a pig. Cock-a-doodle-do like a rooster!

Listen Up!

Say the picture words.

Circle the picture word that begins with the same sound.

TRY IT!

Ask a grown-up to write each letter of the alphabet on small pieces of paper. Pick six of the letters and arrange them in ABC order.

 **U** umbrella			
 **V** valentine			
 **W** wagon			
 **X** x-ray			
 **Y** yo-yo			
 **Z** zebra			

122

Is It Alive?

Circle 4 living things.

TRY IT!

What if animals wore clothes?
Draw some animal clothing, such
as a scarf for a giraffe or shoes
for a chicken.

Activities to Share

Playtime!

Preschoolers love to play. Spark your preschooler's imagination and curiosity with a variety of toys and props. Help your child find creative uses for everyday items. A towel will be a cape for a superhero one minute, then a blanket for a doll the next. Your child will develop fine motor skills by stacking and pushing blocks, boxes, and other objects. Provide a "housekeeping" area for your child, complete with bowls, muffin tins, aprons, measuring cups, and rolling pins.

Word Associations

Cut out pictures from catalogs, magazines, and newspapers on one subject, such as houses. Show your child the pictures and explain that people live in different kinds of houses (big houses, small houses, wooden houses, brick houses, and so on). Discuss how the houses are the same and how they are different. This activity works well with cars, airplanes, people, animals, trees, flowers, clothes, and shoes.

Helping Out

Teach your preschooler responsibility by allowing him or her to help with household chores. Young children can set the table and serve themselves at meals. Your child will enjoy running the vacuum cleaner or raking leaves. Remember that you may have to practice patience when your child is learning how to perform new tasks.

Down on the Farm

Field Trip

Visit a local farm, petting zoo, orchard, or nursery. Your child will enjoy discovering new animals, machinery, and lifestyles.

What Is a Farm?

Discuss with your child why farms are important to people. What do farms produce? Ask your child to think about how farms work. How do farmers keep the animals from wandering away? How do farmers gather the fruits and vegetables when they are ready to be harvested?

Farm Animals

While you are visiting the farm, name all of the animals that you see. Your child will enjoy imitating the noises and behavior of different farm animals.

What Do They Eat?

If possible, watch the animals at the farm while they are being fed. Help your child understand that animals eat different types of food. The horses and the cows may be eating grass in the pastures. The chickens may be eating corn off the ground.

Egg-stimate

Place some plastic eggs under a pillow. Have your child carefully sit on the pillow and guess how many eggs are under it. Then count the eggs with your child.

Farm Art

You and your child can create his or her favorite farm animals from construction paper and some art supplies. Cut a pig from pink construction paper, and then let your child paint "mud" with brown paint. Cut out sheep from white construction paper, and then let your child glue white cotton balls or black yarn on the sheep.

The Spice of Life

Allow your child to taste many different types of cheeses, fruits, and vegetables, even if they aren't your favorites. Remind your child that some foods come from plants and other foods come from animals.

Big Farm Machines

Take your child to look at large farm and construction machines if possible, or select books and videos from the library. You may also be able to find models of tractors, harvesters, and other farm equipment. Tell your child what each machine does, and encourage him or her to think about how machines work.

Activities to Share

Learning at Home

Follow the Lines

On a blank sheet of paper, draw large, looping lines. Ask your child to follow your lines with a crayon. Then allow your child to draw lines for you to trace. Continue the game for as long as you are both having fun. This activity will help your child develop control and use of writing implements—the first step in learning to write letters and numbers.

Matching

Let your child help you with daily matching and sorting tasks, such as putting away groceries or matching pairs of socks. These simple, daily activities reinforce classification and visual discrimination skills.

Big Band Music

You can make "musical instruments" out of pans, wooden spoons, and oatmeal cartons filled with beans. Encourage your child to experiment with different tools and objects that make noise.

Art Starts

Encourage your child to learn through art. Remember, the act of creating is important, not the final artwork. Children enjoy using paper and crayons, but you can also offer unusual art materials, such as coffee filters, aluminum foil, fabric scraps, cardboard paper towel tubes, and yarn.

Nursery Rhymes

You and your child can have fun by changing the words of familiar songs or nursery rhymes to make them silly. For example, make up a rhyme about when Humpty Dumpty went to the store. Or, try singing the song BINGO by spelling your child's name: "K-A-T-H-Y, and Kathy was her name-O!"

It's in the Books

Look closely at the illustrations in your child's favorite books. You may be able to find "extra" stories hidden in the pages. For example, look for animals that aren't characters in the text. Encourage your child to describe why the animals are in the picture, and how they might relate to the main characters.

Counting Toys

Your child can use toy animals to tell a number story. First, ask your child to group his or her toy animals and count them. Ask questions such as the following: How many animals will there be if two more bears come to visit? If one monkey goes away, how many animals will be left?

Always Growing

Keep a record of your child's height by marking the wall and measuring his or her height every two weeks or every month. Young children enjoy seeing how big they are. Encourage your child to compare his or her height to other objects, such as a favorite chair. Challenge your child to predict how tall he or she will be next year. The marks on the wall are a graph of your child's growth.

How Things Move

When you are outside, ask your child to look for different animals and to watch how they move. Some animals crawl, some slither, and some fly. Make a list of the animals you observed and categorize them according to how they move.

Light as a Feather

Allow your child to examine some feathers with a magnifying glass. Ask your child to feel the weight of a feather. Can he or she find anything that is as light as a feather? Encourage your child to play with the feather, to see how it behaves in a breeze and when it is dropped. Do feathers float in water?

Write Lists

To show your child the importance of written words, allow him or her to write items on a shopping list. Encourage your child to sound out the first letter of each word that needs to be written on the list. For example, if you need to purchase soap, say the word and ask your child to identify the beginning sound.

Sand Play

Let your child spend time playing in the sand. Offer him or her plastic containers, spoons, a sieve, and pans. Children learn about the world around them by feeling the sand, watching how it reacts to water, and seeing how tools can be used to manipulate it.

Resource Guide

Flash Action Colors, Shapes & More

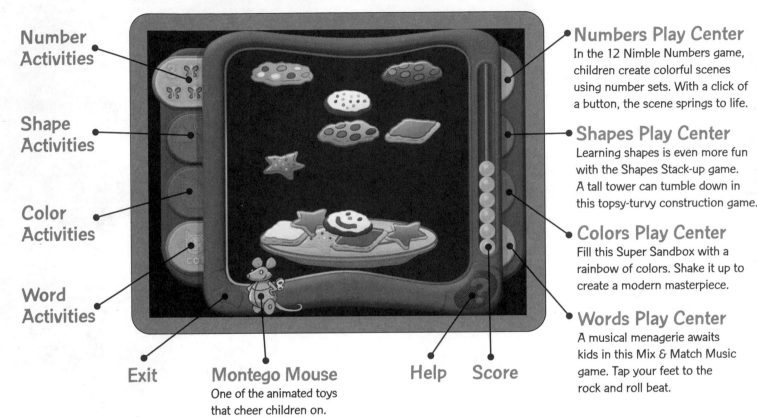

Number Activities

Shape Activities

Color Activities

Word Activities

Exit

Montego Mouse
One of the animated toys that cheer children on.

Help   **Score**

Numbers Play Center
In the 12 Nimble Numbers game, children create colorful scenes using number sets. With a click of a button, the scene springs to life.

Shapes Play Center
Learning shapes is even more fun with the Shapes Stack-up game. A tall tower can tumble down in this topsy-turvy construction game.

Colors Play Center
Fill this Super Sandbox with a rainbow of colors. Shake it up to create a modern masterpiece.

Words Play Center
A musical menagerie awaits kids in this Mix & Match Music game. Tap your feet to the rock and roll beat.

Preschoolers will listen, laugh, and learn as they discover important skills through play and practice. In this delightful CD-ROM, some very talented toys cheer children on as they practice colors, shapes, numbers, and more. Four unique Play Centers provide positive reinforcement of newly learned concepts. Bright colors, imaginative characters, and silly sound effects add kid-appeal to make learning beginning skills child's play.

Educational Goal
To introduce and practice important preschool skills through a variety of fun activities, and then to reinforce those skills through constructive games.

Educational Content
- Numbers
- Shapes
- Colors
- Classification
- Positional Words
- Rhyming

Developmental Skills
- Following Directions
- Eye-hand Coordination
- Critical Thinking
- Problem Solving
- Listening
- Creativity
- Exploration

Program Features
- Learning is reinforced with audio and animated rewards.
- The simple program design allows children to work independently.
- Learned concepts are reinforced through creative Play Centers.
- Play Centers allow children to influence their environment and encourage exploration and creativity.
- Bright colors, adorable characters, and silly sound effects appeal to children.

Flash Action Preschool Software & Workbook Combo **08151**